9|15 OX

WHAT IS CITIZENSHIP?

Leslie Harper

BELLWOOD PUBLIC LIBRARY

PowerKiDS press™
New York

Published in 2013 by The Rosen Publishing Group, Inc.
29 East 21st Street, New York, NY 10010

First Edition

Editor: Jennifer Way
Book Design: Ashley Drago
Layout Design: Andrew Povolny

Photo Credits: pp. 4–5 Monkey Business Images/Shutterstock.com; p. 6 Lambert/Archive Photos/Getty Images; p. 7 Lewis W. Hine/Museum of the City of New York/Archive Photos/Getty Images; p. 8 Yuri Arcurs/Shutterstock.com; p. 9 iStockphoto/Thinkstock; pp. 10–11 Stockbyte/Thinkstock; p. 12 Chris Hondros/Getty Images; p. 13 Richard Ellis/Getty Images; pp. 14–15 Michael Nagle/Getty Images; p. 16 © iStockphoto/Moodboard_Images; p. 17 Hulton Archive/Getty Images; p. 18 Jupiterimages/Workbook Stock/Getty Images; p. 19 Stockbyte/Thinkstock; pp. 20–21 Digital Vision/Thinkstock.

Library of Congress Cataloging-in-Publication Data

Harper, Leslie.
 What is citizenship? / by Leslie Harper. — 1st ed.
    p. cm. — (Civics Q&A)
 Includes index.
 ISBN 978-1-4488-7435-4 (library binding) — ISBN 978-1-4488-7508-5 (pbk.) —
 ISBN 978-1-4488-7582-5 (6-pack)
 1. Citizenship—United States—Juvenile literature. I. Title.
 JK1759.H247 2013
 323.60973—dc23
                              2012000387

Manufactured in the United States of America

CPSIA Compliance Information: Batch #SW12PK: For Further Information contact Rosen Publishing, New York, New York at 1-800-237-9932

CONTENTS

WHAT IS CITIZENSHIP?

A **citizen** is someone who is born in a country or has a lawful right to live there. Citizens have certain rights and **responsibilities** to other people around them. When people act as good citizens, it is easier for everyone to get along as a community and as a country.

There are two ways to become a citizen of the United States. A person can be born a citizen or can become one by law. A person who was born in another country and becomes a US citizen by law is called a **naturalized** citizen.

Americans celebrate their country on Independence Day. It is also a day many people think about what citizenship means to them.

5

A NATION OF IMMIGRANTS

The Pilgrims who came to America on the *Mayflower* were immigrants and colonists. Each wave of settlers since has helped make the United States the nation of immigrants it is today.

Have you ever moved? Sometimes people move for work, to be closer to relatives, or because the place they live is dangerous. A person who moves from one country to another is called an **immigrant**.

The United States is often called a nation of immigrants. When European settlers arrived in North America, the only other people living there were Native Americans. That means that European settlers and everyone who came after them were immigrants in different ways! Your family may have come to the United States hundreds of years ago or they might have come in just the last few years.

In the late 1800s and early 1900s, many immigrants came into the United States through Ellis Island, in New York, shown here.

WHAT IS AN ALIEN?

People come to the United States from all over the world to work. They must have permission to live and work in the United States, though.

When talking about citizenship, an **alien** is someone who is a citizen of one country but who lives in another country. Many aliens who live in the United States are here legally. They have permission to work in the United States. They may also own property. They have many of the same rights as citizens.

However, some aliens are people who are in the United States illegally. They do not have permission to work, though many do. If the government catches an illegal alien, he may be **deported**, or sent back to his own country.

Students may come to the United States to study at a college or university. They need to have permission to go to school in the United States.

What Is a Natural-Born Citizen?

People born in the United States are called **natural-born citizens**. That means there is nothing that they must do to become citizens. If one or both of a child's parents are US citizens, then that child is a natural-born US citizen, too. This is true even if children are born while their parents are in another country.

In most cases, naturalized citizens have all of the same rights as natural-born citizens. However, natural-born citizens have one special right. The US **Constitution** says that a person must be a natural-born citizen to become the president of the United States.

A natural-born citizen is someone who is a US citizen at birth. This may be because his parents are American or because he was born in the United States.

WHAT IS NATURALIZED CITIZENSHIP?

These people are being sworn in as new US citizens.

A naturalized citizen is someone who was not born a US citizen but becomes one by law. To become a citizen, a person must live in the United States legally for at least five years. People must show that they know how to speak, read, and write English.

To become naturalized citizens, people must also take a test to prove they know about important events in US history and they understand how the US government works.

Becoming a naturalized citizen is not easy. However, most people do it because they want to take part in the rights and responsibilities of their new country!

This woman is holding the certificate she was given at her naturalization ceremony.

NEW CITIZENS

The final step in becoming a new citizen is a naturalization **ceremony**, or service. At the ceremony, new citizens will take an **oath**, or make a promise, to be loyal to the United States. They promise to support the Constitution and all laws. The new citizens will usually say the **Pledge of Allegiance**, too.

Citizenship ceremonies celebrate and welcome new citizens. At the ceremony, people often give speeches about the importance of citizenship. New citizens are given a copy of the Constitution and a small American flag. These naturalized citizens now have the same rights and responsibilities as natural-born citizens!

The naturalization ceremony is an exciting day for new citizens and their families. This ceremony was held at the Statue of Liberty, in New York, in 2011.

WHAT ARE CITIZENS' RIGHTS?

A right is something that everyone should be allowed to do. Citizens of the United States have several important rights. Many of these rights are found in the Bill of Rights, a list of the first 10 **amendments**, or changes, to the Constitution.

Citizens have a right to a trial by jury. Adult citizens have a responsibility to serve on juries when they are called to do so.

The Bill of Rights gives all citizens the freedom of speech and the right to gather together peacefully. This right allows people to disagree with the government publicly without fear of being arrested. People also have the right to belong to any religion they want, the right to a fair trial, and many other important rights.

Martin Luther King Jr. fought for African Americans to have the same civil rights as everyone else. Civil rights are rights that all citizens share.

WHAT ARE CITIZENS' RESPONSIBILITIES?

Voting is both a right and a responsibility. It is one way that citizens can have an effect on their country.

Citizens have important responsibilities to their country. Responsibilities are things that people must do for our country to keep it running. For example, all citizens, even kids, have a responsibility to obey the law.

One of the most important responsibilities that citizens have is voting. Adults can vote for who will serve in the national, state, and local governments. Citizens also have a responsibility to serve in the military if they are asked to by the government.

Paying taxes is a very important responsibility. Tax money helps the government provide firefighters, police officers, public schools, and many other important things.

Many people feel it is their responsibility to their country to join the military without being asked to by the government.

A MELTING POT

US citizens come from many different **cultures**. We have many different ideas, beliefs, and values. For this reason, the United States is often called a melting pot. People from many different backgrounds come together, or "melt," to create one society.

For hundreds of years, immigrants from Ireland, China, Italy, Mexico, and many other countries all over the world have brought parts of their cultures to the United States. Music, food, art, and language have all been touched by immigration. As new citizens continue to come into the United States, our culture will continue to grow and change.

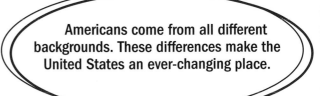
Americans come from all different backgrounds. These differences make the United States an ever-changing place.

CITIZENSHIP Q&A

1

Q: Where do many legal immigrants to the United States come from today?

A: **Most legal immigrants come to the United States from Mexico, China, India, and the Philippines.**

2

Q: What is Ellis Island?

A: **Ellis Island, near New York City, was the immigration station where most immigrants entered the United States between 1892 and 1954.**

3

Q: What is a visa?

A: **A visa is a piece of paper or a stamp in a passport that says a person has permission to enter a country. The United States has both visas for immigrants and visas for people who are just visiting.**

4

Q: What is dual citizenship?

A: **Dual citizenship is when a person is a citizen of two countries at the same time.**

5

Q: What part of the government deals with immigration and citizenship?

A: **A department called US Citizen and Immigration Services, or USCIS, deals with legal immigration to the United States.**

6

Q: What is a green card?

A: **A green card is a card that says that someone is a legal permanent resident of the United States.**

GLOSSARY

alien (AY-lee-un) A person who is a citizen of one country but lives in another.

amendments (uh-MEND-ments) Additions or changes to the Constitution.

ceremony (SER-ih-moh-nee) A special action done on certain occasions.

citizen (SIH-tih-zen) A person who was born in or has a right to live in a country or other community.

Constitution (kon-stih-TOO-shun) The basic rules by which the United States is governed.

cultures (KUL-churz) The beliefs, practices, and arts of groups of people.

deported (dih-PORT-ed) Sent out of a country.

immigrant (IH-muh-grunt) Someone who moves to a new country from another country.

natural-born citizens (NA-chuh-rul-born SIH-tih-zenz) People who are born US citizens. This includes people born in the United States and people born outside the United States with one or two parents who are US citizens.

naturalized (NA-chuh-ruh-lyzd) Became a citizen.

oath (OHTH) A promise.

Pledge of Allegiance (PLEJ UV uh-LEE-jents) An expression of loyalty to the United States and its flag.

responsibilities (rih-spon-sih-BIH-lih-teez) Things that people must take care of or complete.

INDEX

WEBSITES

Due to the changing nature of Internet links, PowerKids Press has developed an online list of websites related to the subject of this book. This site is updated regularly. Please use this link to access the list:
www.powerkidslinks.com/civ/cit/